Alphabet Album

by Jeanette Stone Crews

Leisure Arts Inc. • Maumelle Arkansas

INTRODUCTION

These decorative alphabets were compiled to bring you an assortment of styles and sizes to fit any need. We have included upper case, lower case and numbers in most of the styles. There are alphabets for backstitch only, some that are cross stitch with backstitch and some that have no backstitch - suitable for needlepoint.

Jeanette Stone Crews is from Atlanta, Georgia, and has been designing needlework for over 5 years. She is a member of the Georgia Embroiderer's Guild, and was a charter member of the Charleston, South Carolina Embroiderer's Guild.

Several alphabets were designed by Karen Uhlich Bowdish and Amy Stallings Skelton. Amy is from Tuscaloosa, Alabama, and has been designing needlework for about 1 year. She is Jeanette's niece. Karen is from Atlanta and is a graduate of the Chicago Art Institute. She is also a member of the Georgia Embroiderer's Guild.

We hope you find many uses for these Alphabets and enjoy stitching them.

Cover items made and patterns tested by Susan Barrs, Brenda Cantrell, Debbie Cleary, Bobbie Graham, Nell Harris, Barbara Herring, Mildred Huff, Kay Kilbury, Kay Magness, Nancy Malitz, Joanne McLendon, Bettiemae Moon, Julia Penaloza, Carmen Puckett, Sue Sayles and Linda Vikla.

Made in U.S.A.

TABLE OF CONTENTS

GENERAL INSTRUCTIONS

WORKING WITH CHARTS

How To Read Charts: Each of the Alphabets is shown in chart form. Each square on the chart represents one needlework stitch, whether it be a needlepoint tent stitch or complete cross stitch. The straight lines on the chart indicate Backstitching; these lines are shown in black.

Basic Thread Counts

Needlepoint Canvas:	10, 12, 13, 14 and 18 are most common
Aida:	11, 14, 18 per inch
Hardanger:	22 per inch (sometimes worked over 2 threads in which case 11 per inch)

If working on an unlabeled canvas or fabric, simply measure and count the number of threads that fall within an inch.

Where To Start: Find the center of your design by counting the number of squares horizontally and vertically and dividing each by 2. The resulting point is your center. You may start at any point, but be sure to allow plenty of margin. It is better to waste a little fabric than to come up short after hours of stitching!

A blank piece of graph paper has been included in this leaflet for your convenience in charting your designs.

STITCHING TIPS

Preparing Fabric or Canvas: Bind raw edges of canvas with tape; overcast raw edges of fabric. Locate horizontal and vertical centers by folding your canvas or fabric in half, top to bottom and again right to left.

Preparing Thread: When working with stranded yarn or threads, separate, then realign them before threading needle. This gives you a smoother stitch. For ease in stitching, you may thread a needle with each color to be used; lead thread away from working area and anchor needle in top of work until color is required again. Keep stitching tension consistent. Begin and end working threads by running under several stitches on back; never tie knots.

Counted Cross Stitch: Work one cross stitch to correspond to each square on the chart. Use the "stab stitch" method of stitching, bringing needle up at odd numbers and down at even numbers. For horizontal rows, work stitches in two journeys ***(Fig. 1)***. For vertical rows, complete each stitch as shown ***(Fig. 2)***. When working on Hardanger over 2 threads, work cross stitch as in **Fig. 3**.

Fig. 1

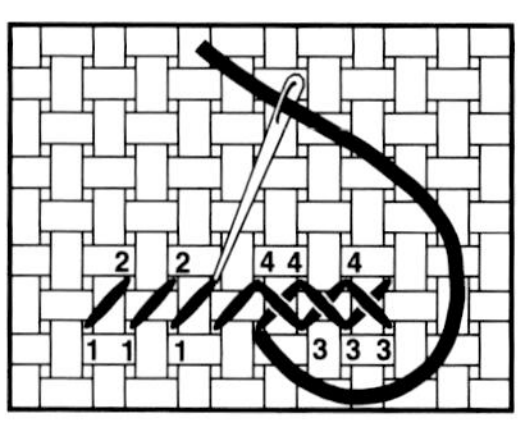

Fig. 2

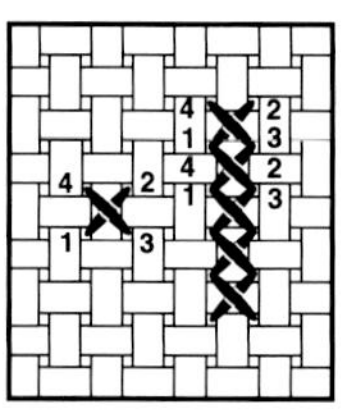

Fig. 3

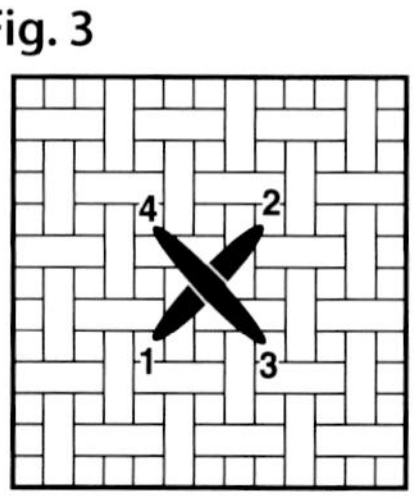

Needlepoint: Work a tent stitch to correspond to each square on the chart. When working a single row of tent stitches horizontally, vertically or diagonally, use the Continental method (**Fig. 4**). When working an area having several rows of stitches, use the Diagonal Tent (Basketweave) method (**Fig. 5**).

Fig. 4

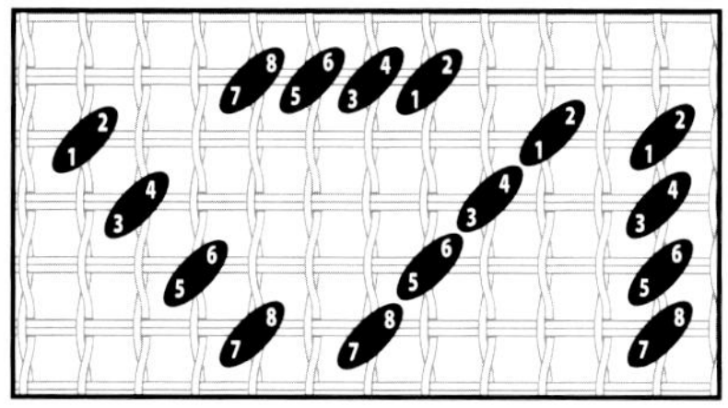

Fig. 5

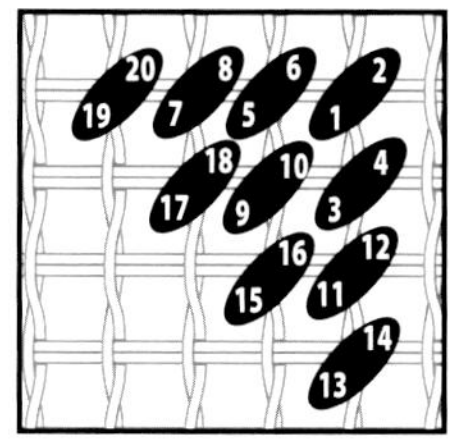

Backstitching: Outline detail shown by dark straight lines should be worked by Backstitching ***(Fig. 6)*** after the needlepoint ***(Fig. 7)*** or cross stitch design has been completed. Backstitch for Hardanger over 2 is shown in **Fig. 8**. In some Alphabet styles, the backstitching forms the whole alphabet. In other cases it is used with complete stitches.

fig. 6

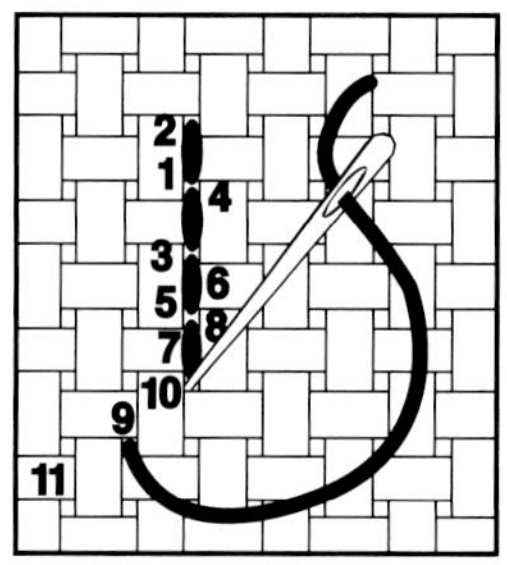

fig. 7

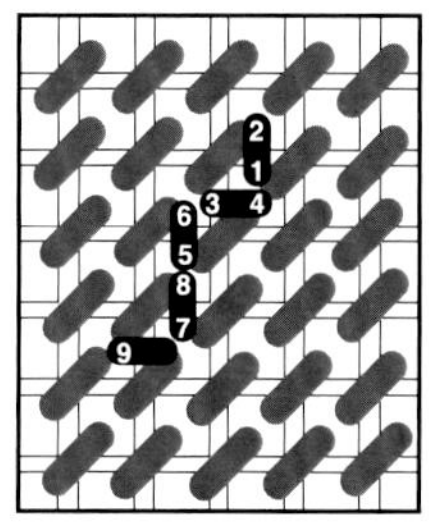

Fig. 8

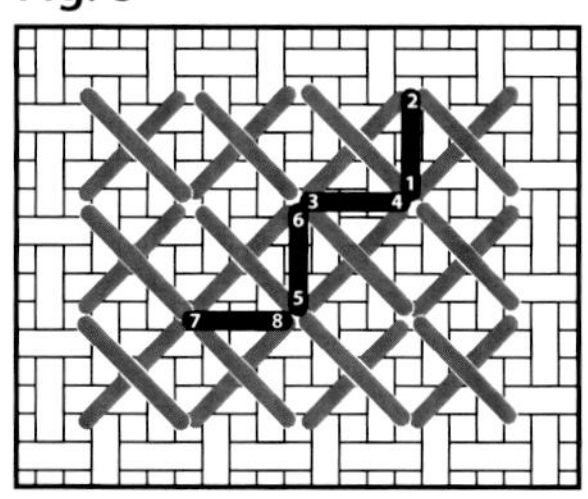

Yarn and Floss Thickness: Recommended yarn or floss thickness is as follows. This is merely a suggestion, especially where backstitching is concerned. Experiment to get the look you desire.

12-14 mesh Canvas	2 strands persian or 1 strand tapestry (lightweight) for tent stitch; 1 strand persian or 2-3 strands embroidery floss for backstitch
Aida 11 or Hardanger Over 2	2-3 strands floss for cross stitch; 2-3 strands for backstitch
Aida 18 and Hardanger	1 strand for cross stitch; 1 strand for backstitch.

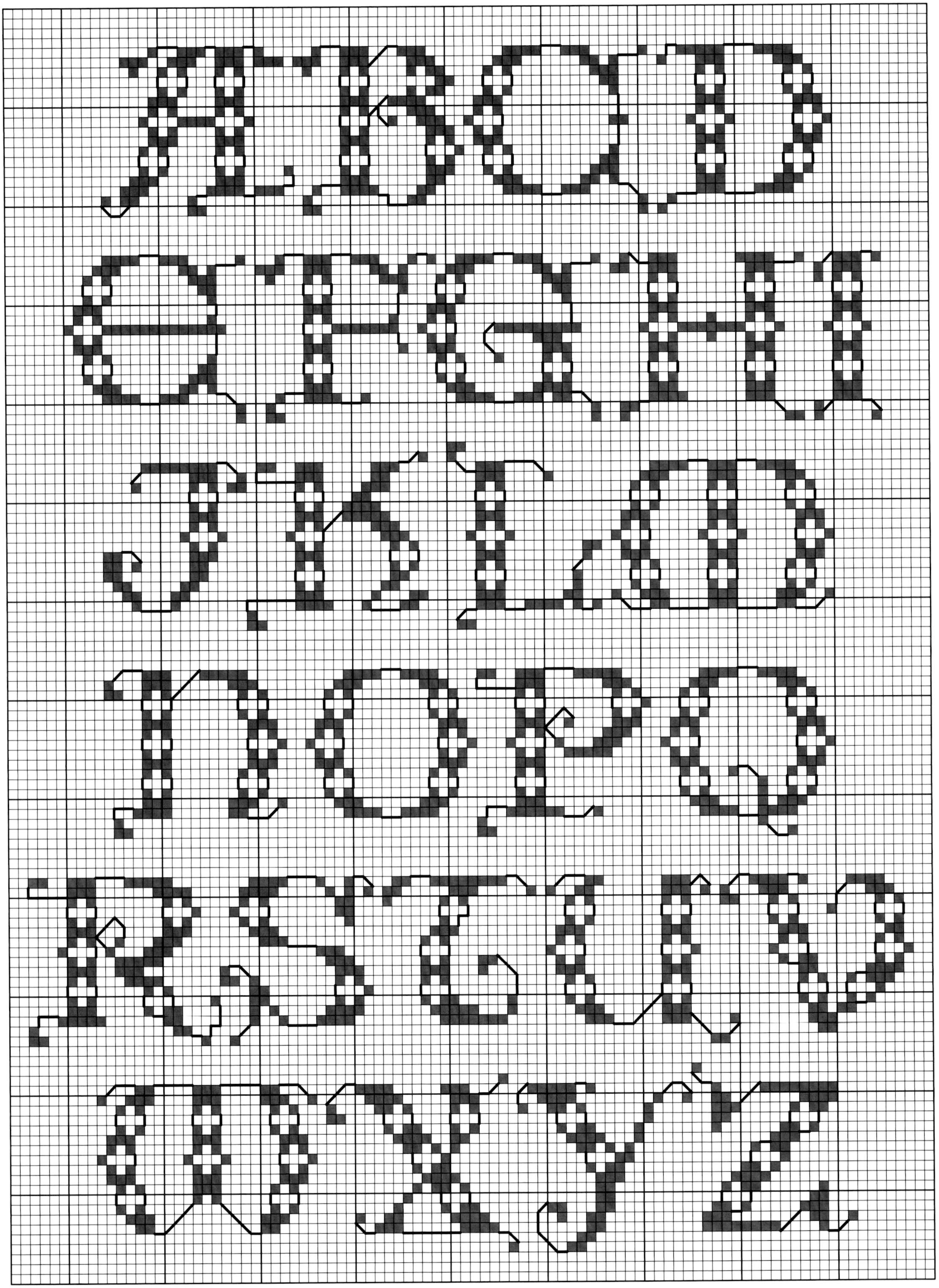

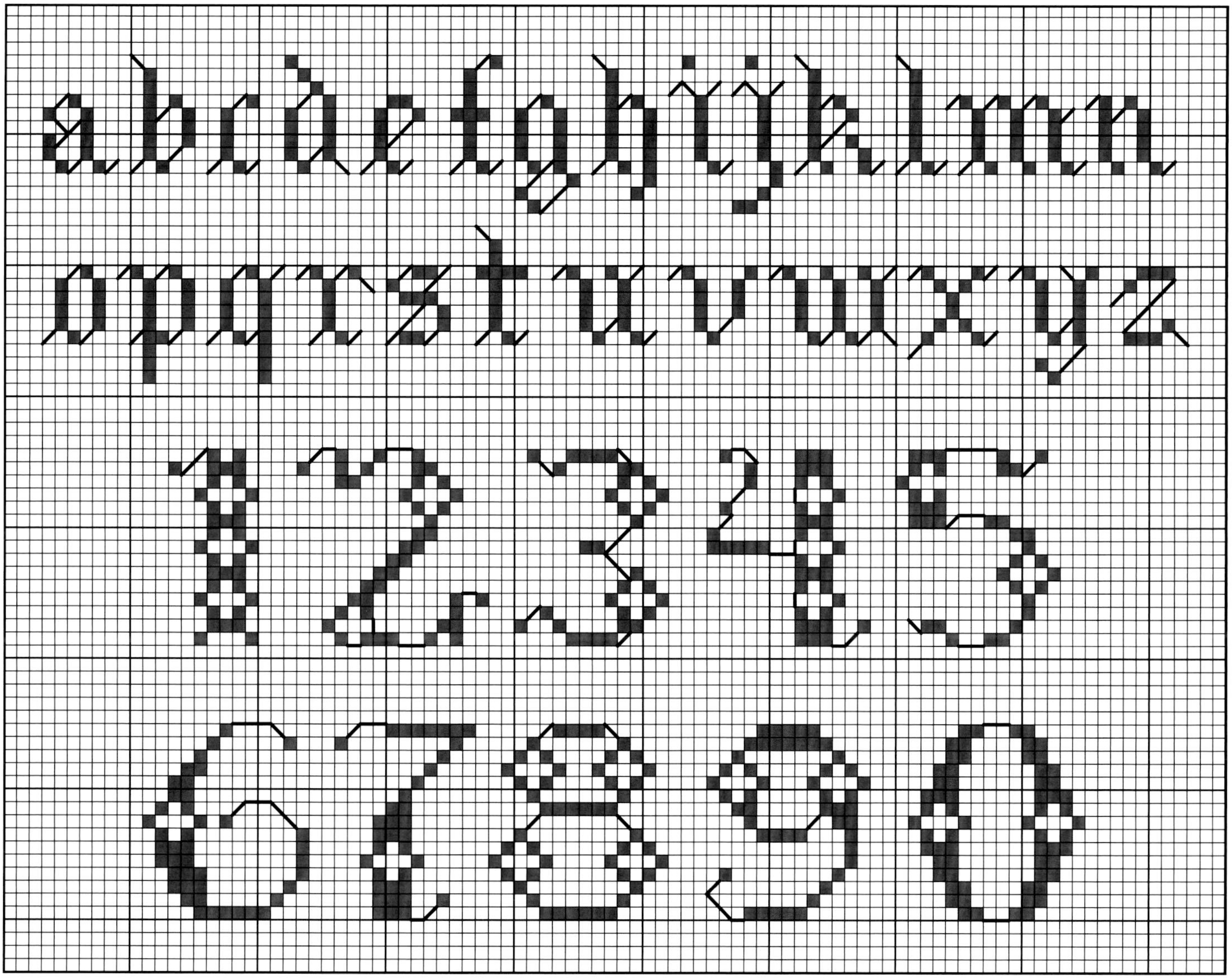

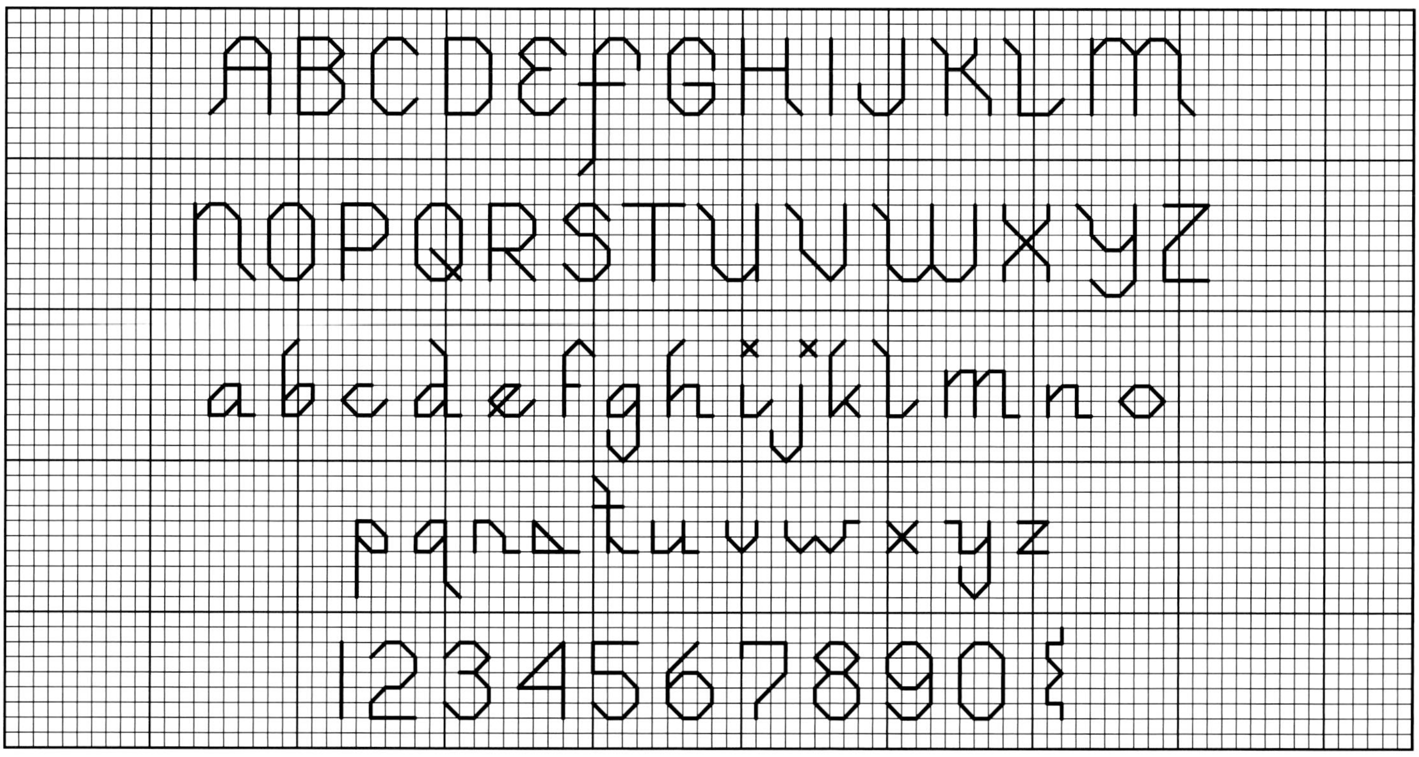

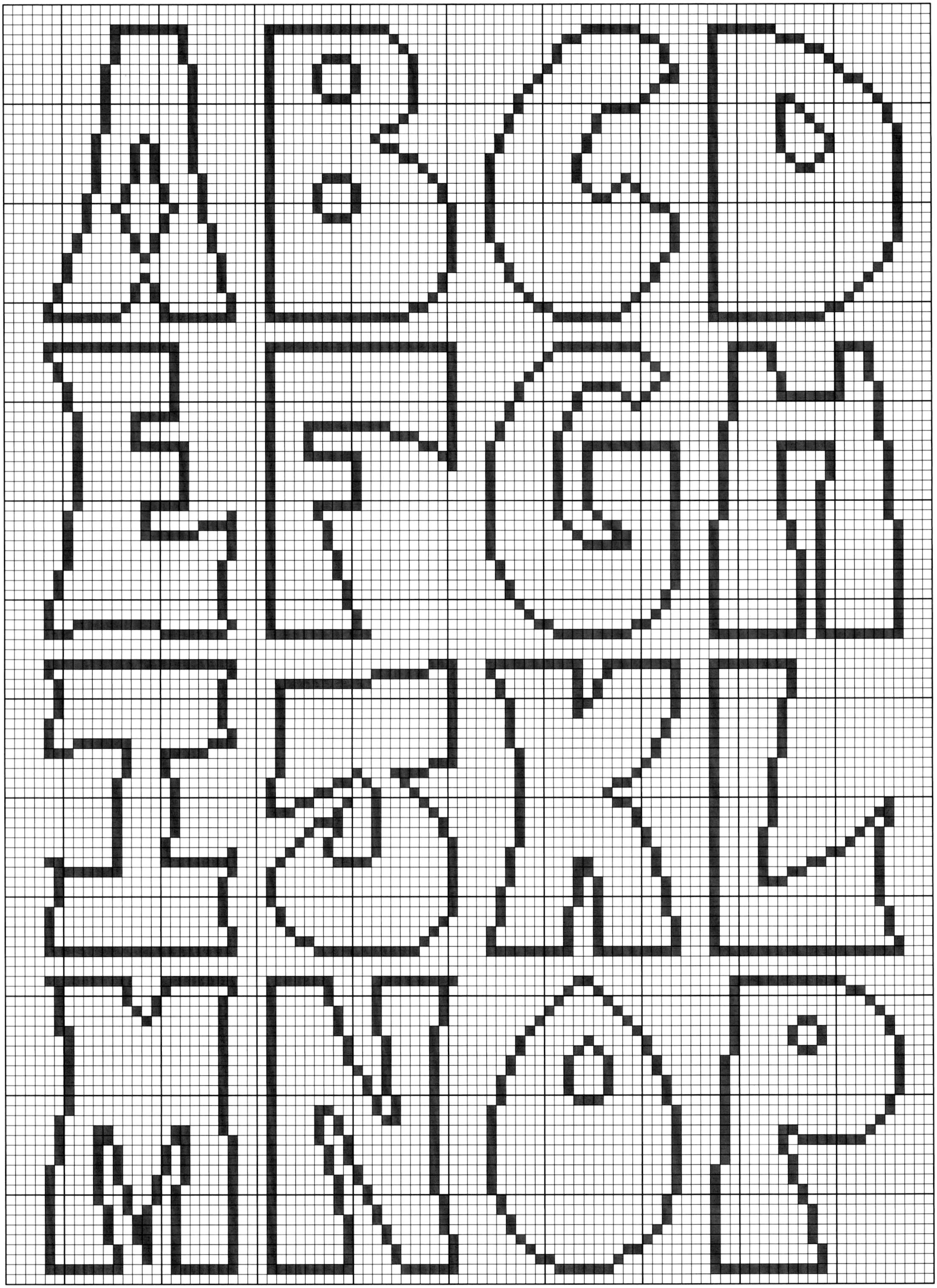

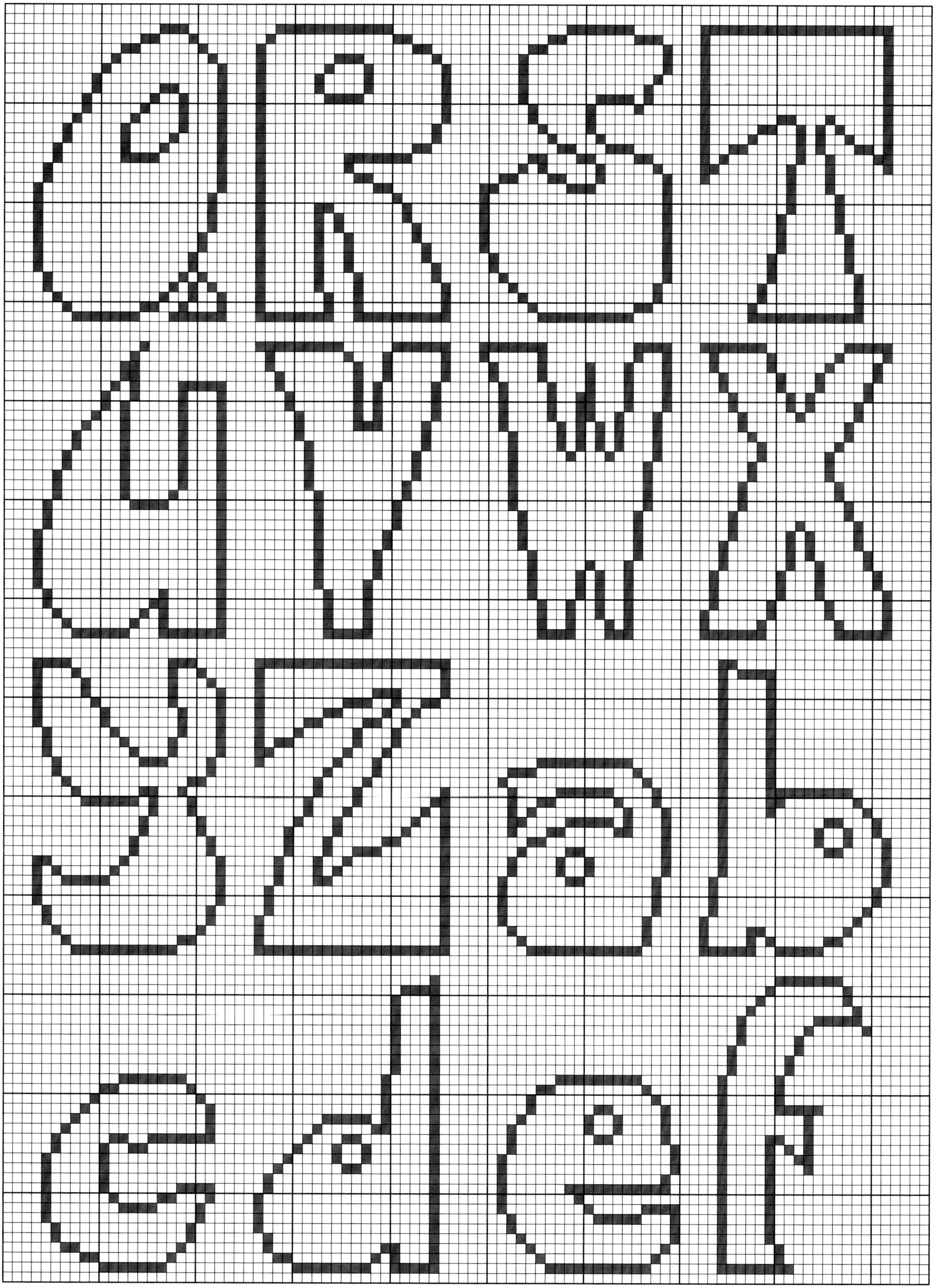

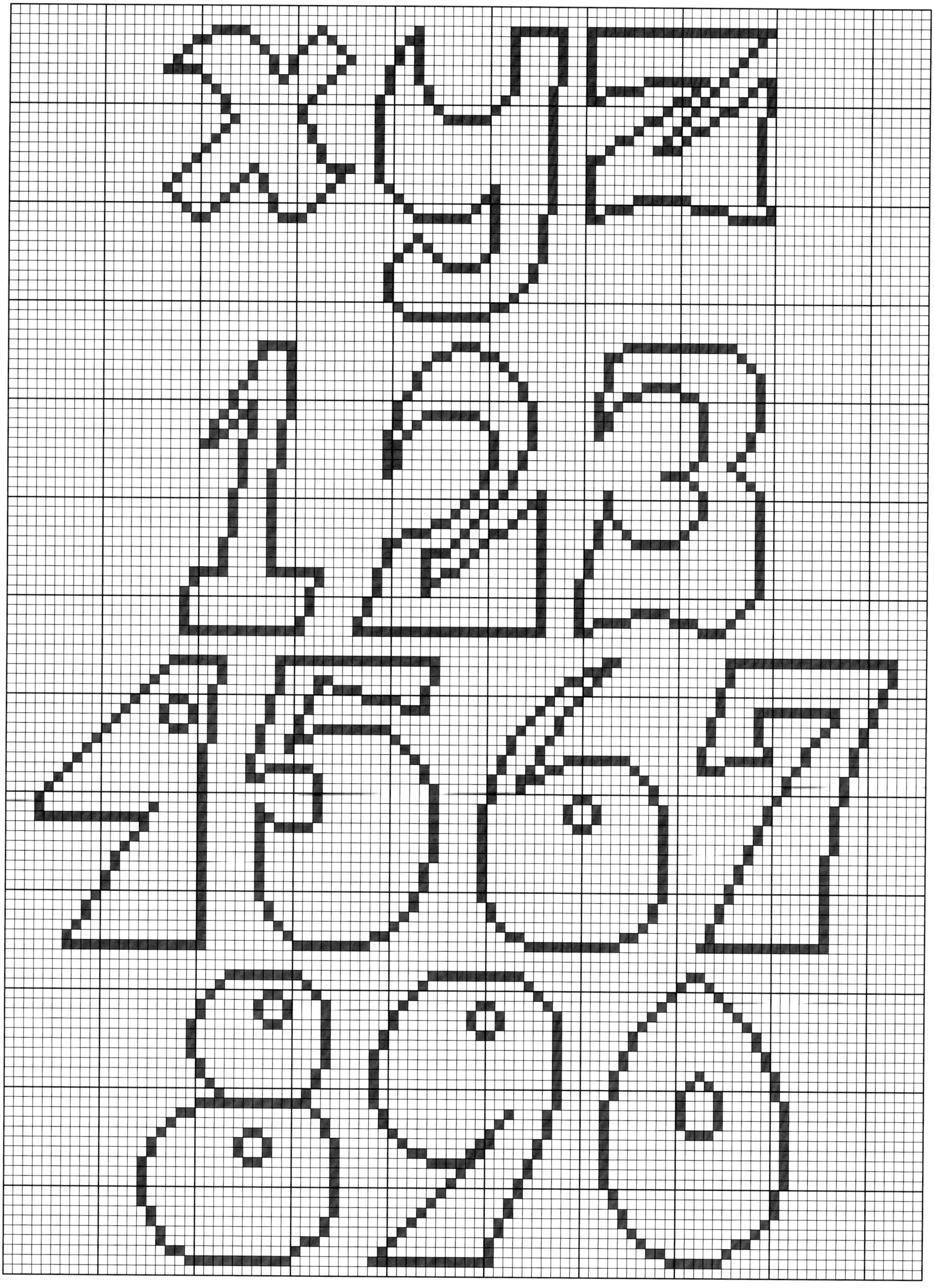

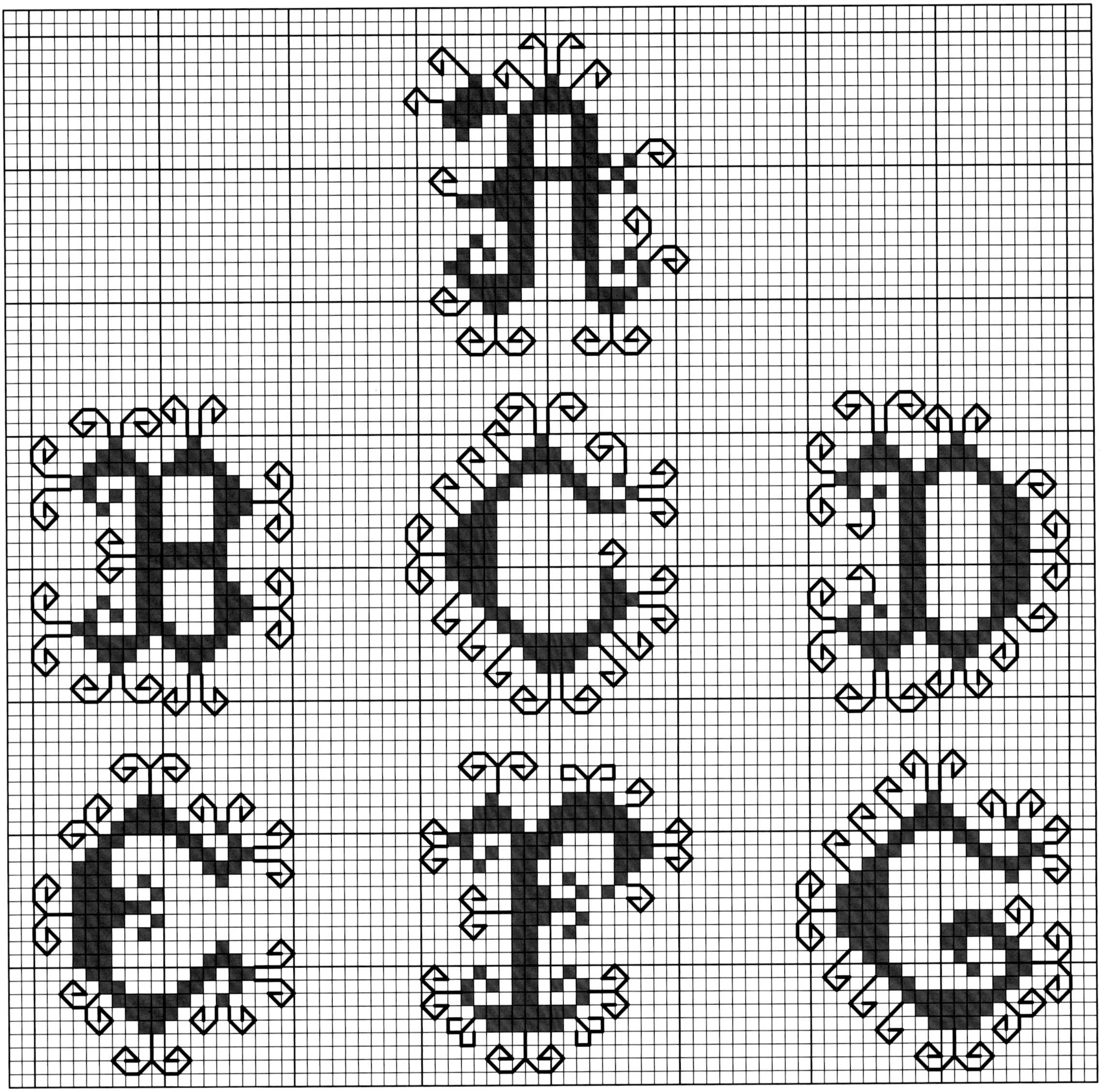

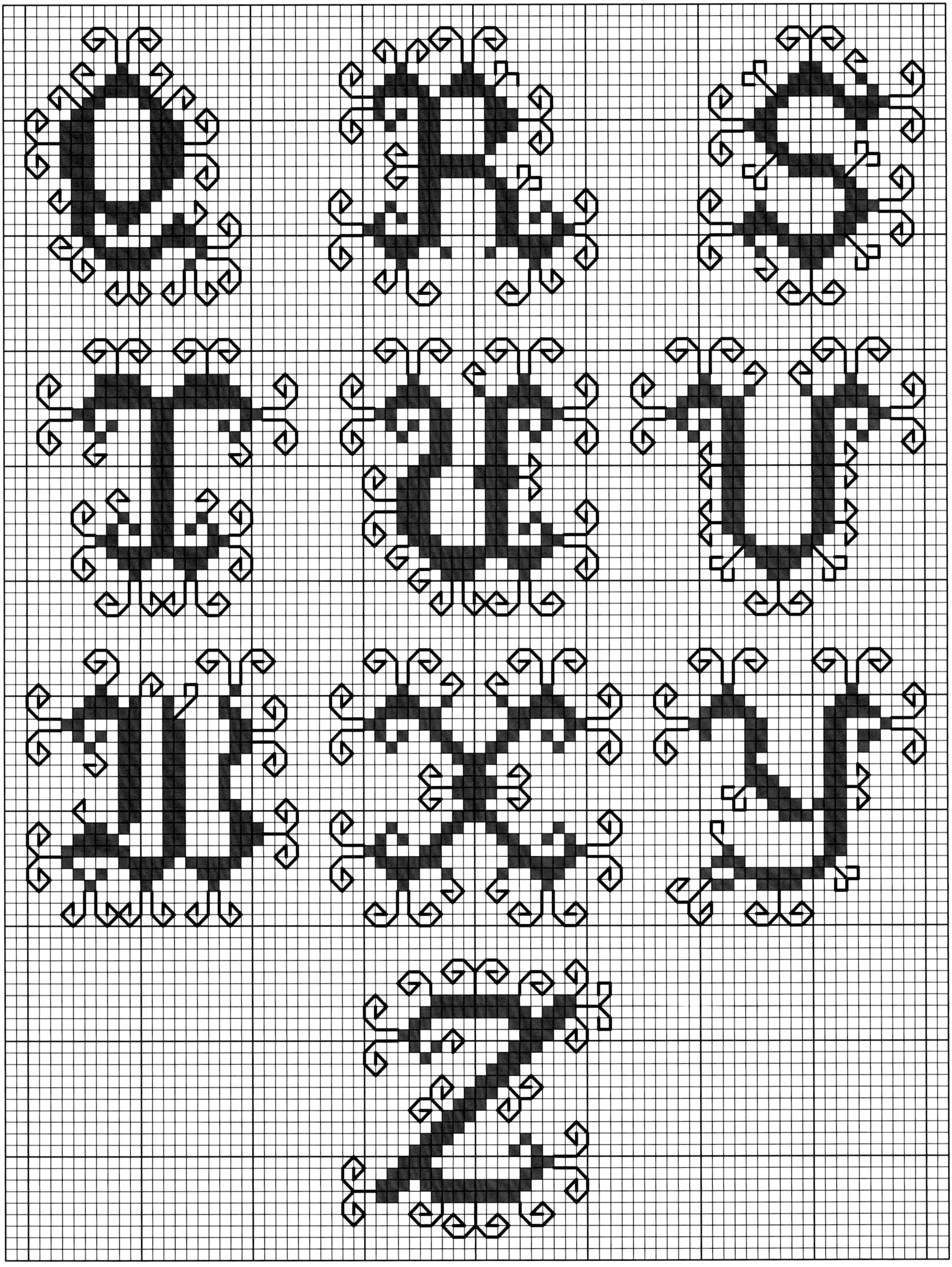

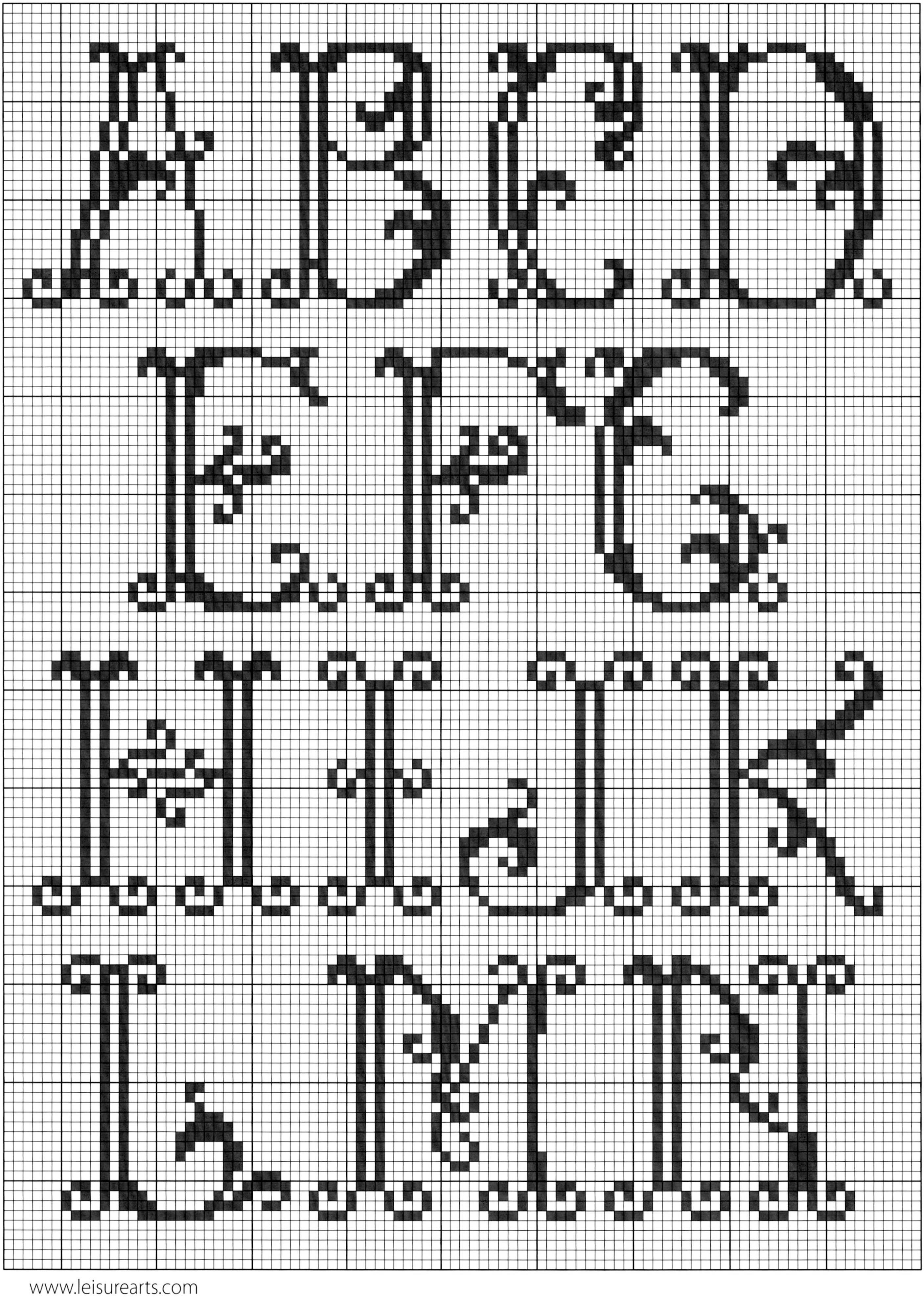

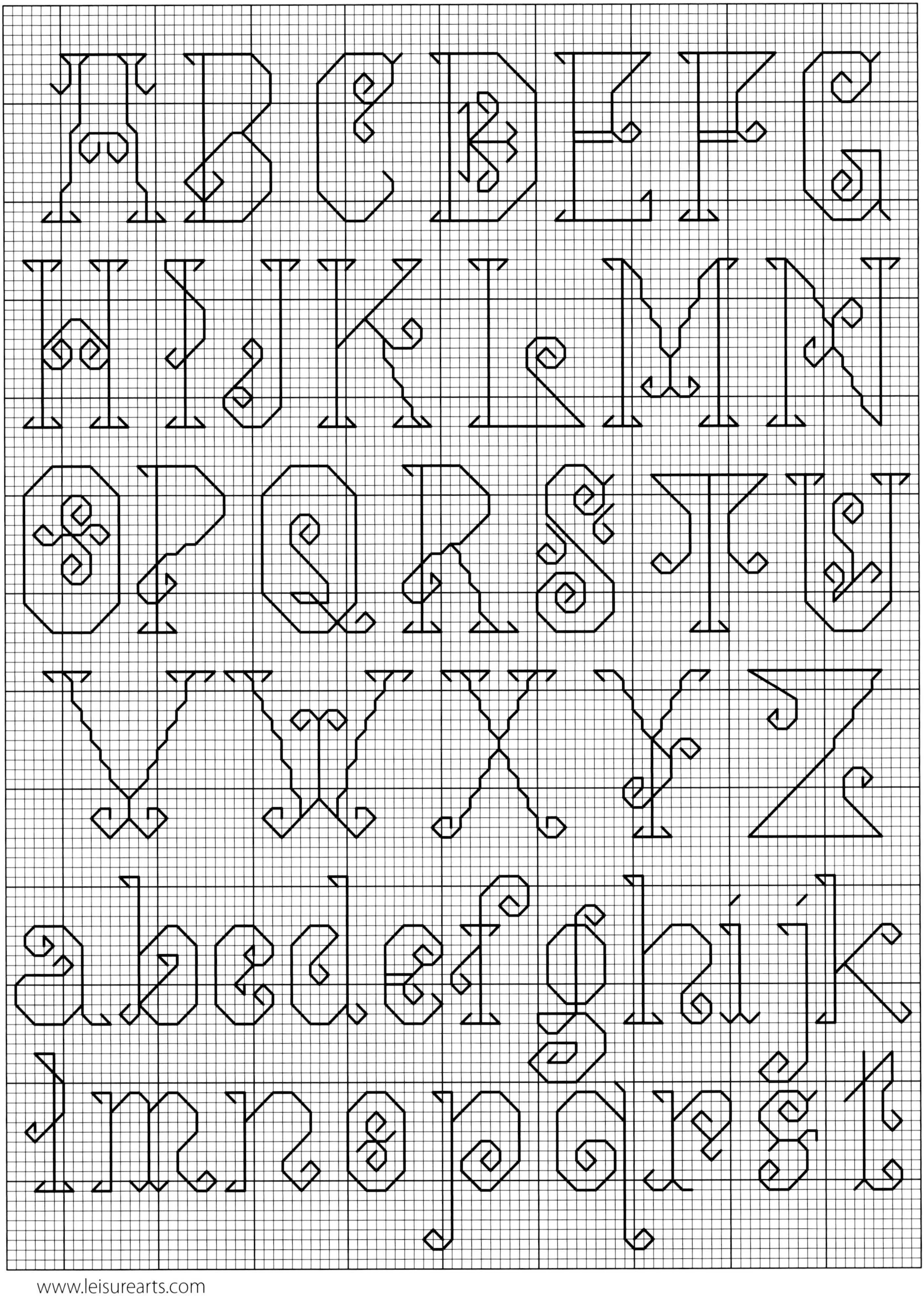

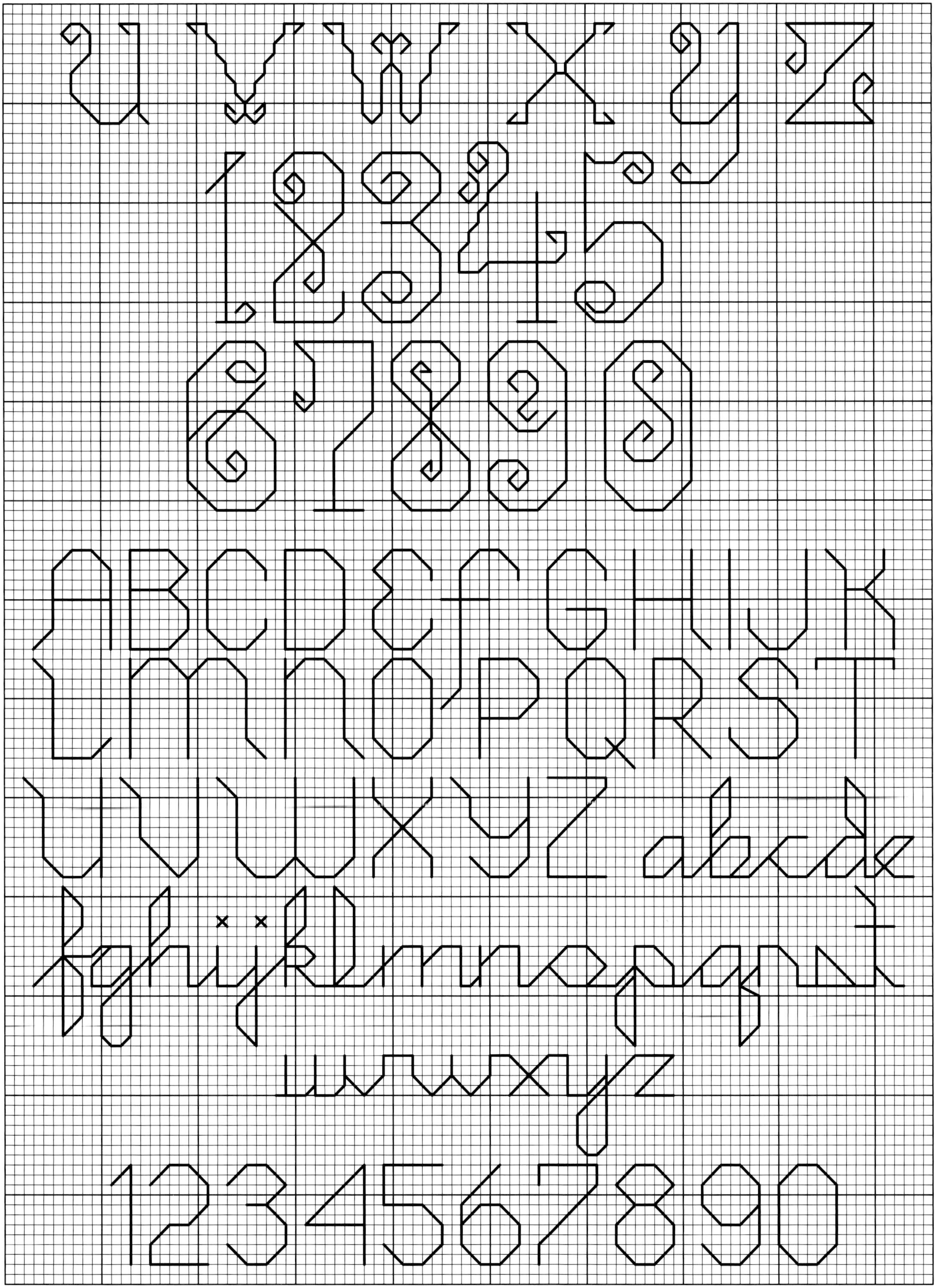

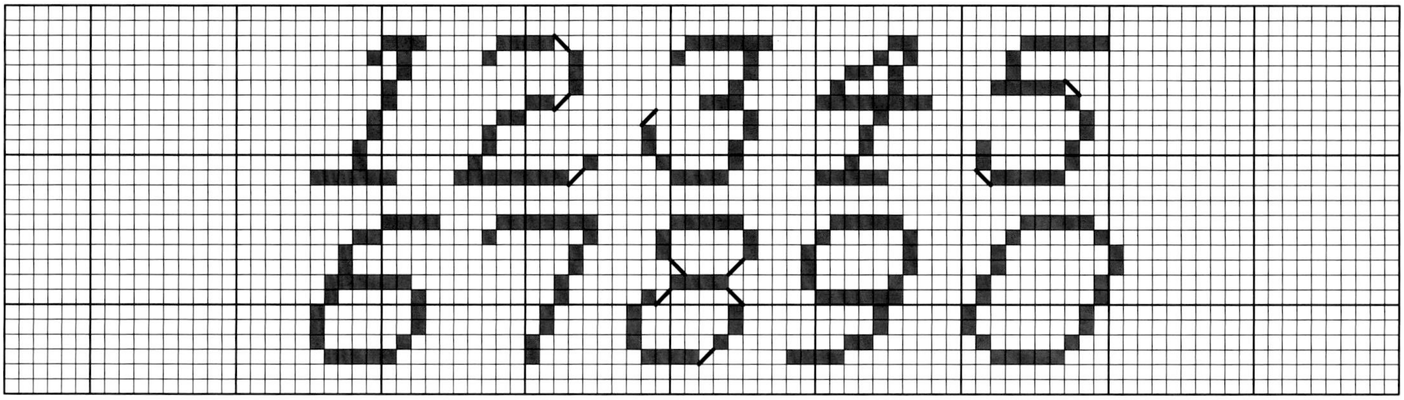

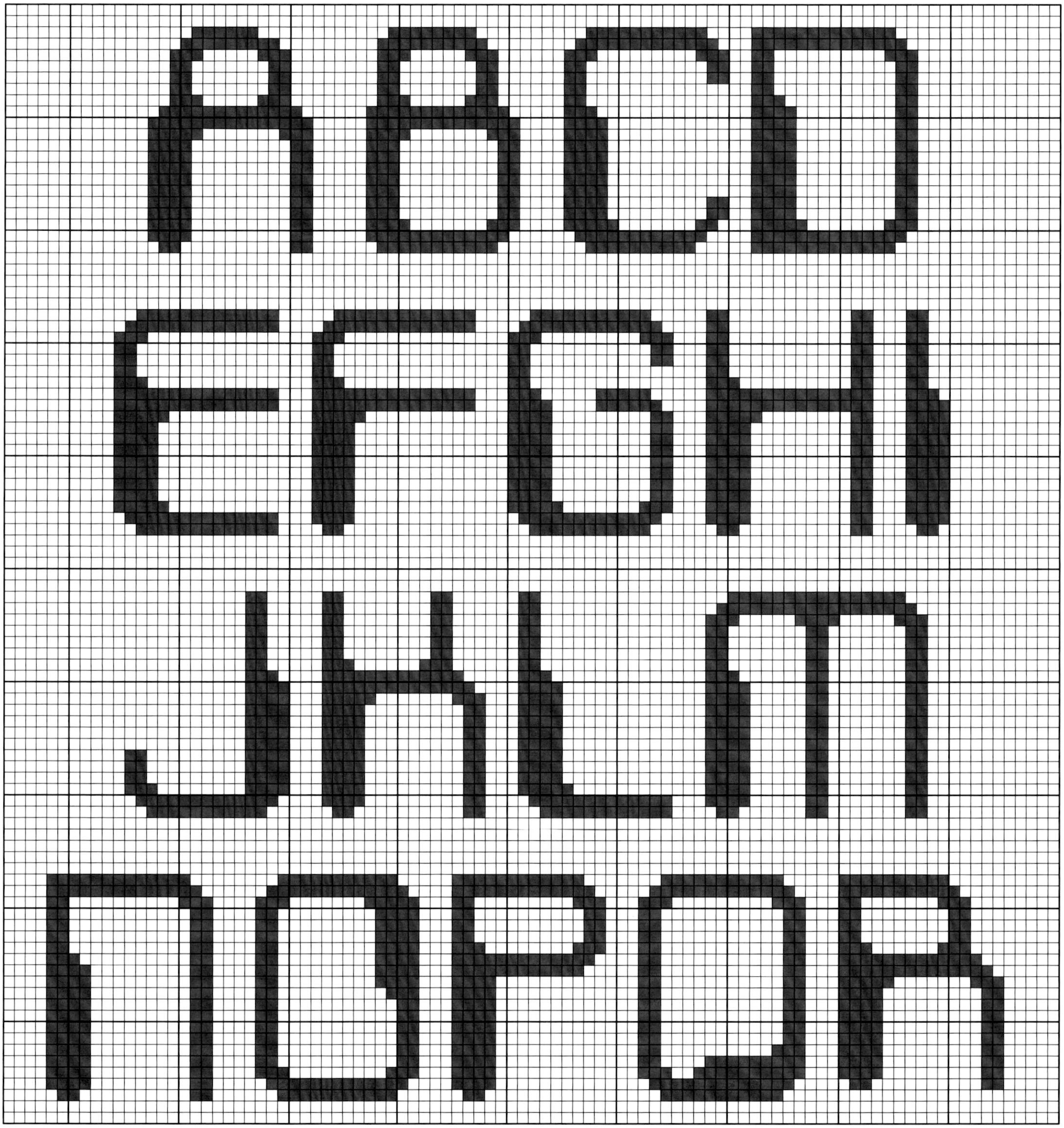

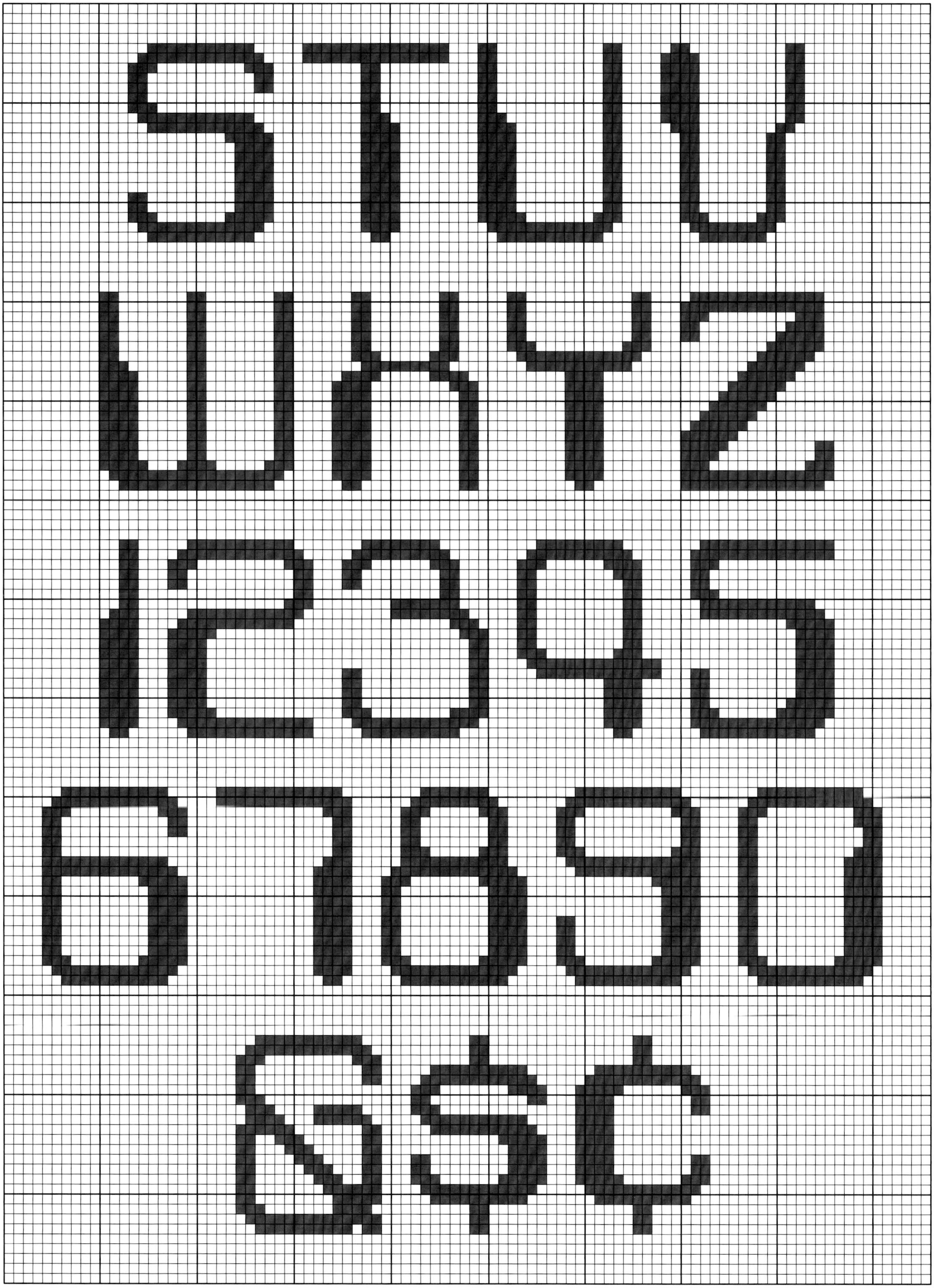
STUV
WXYZ
12345
67890
&$¢

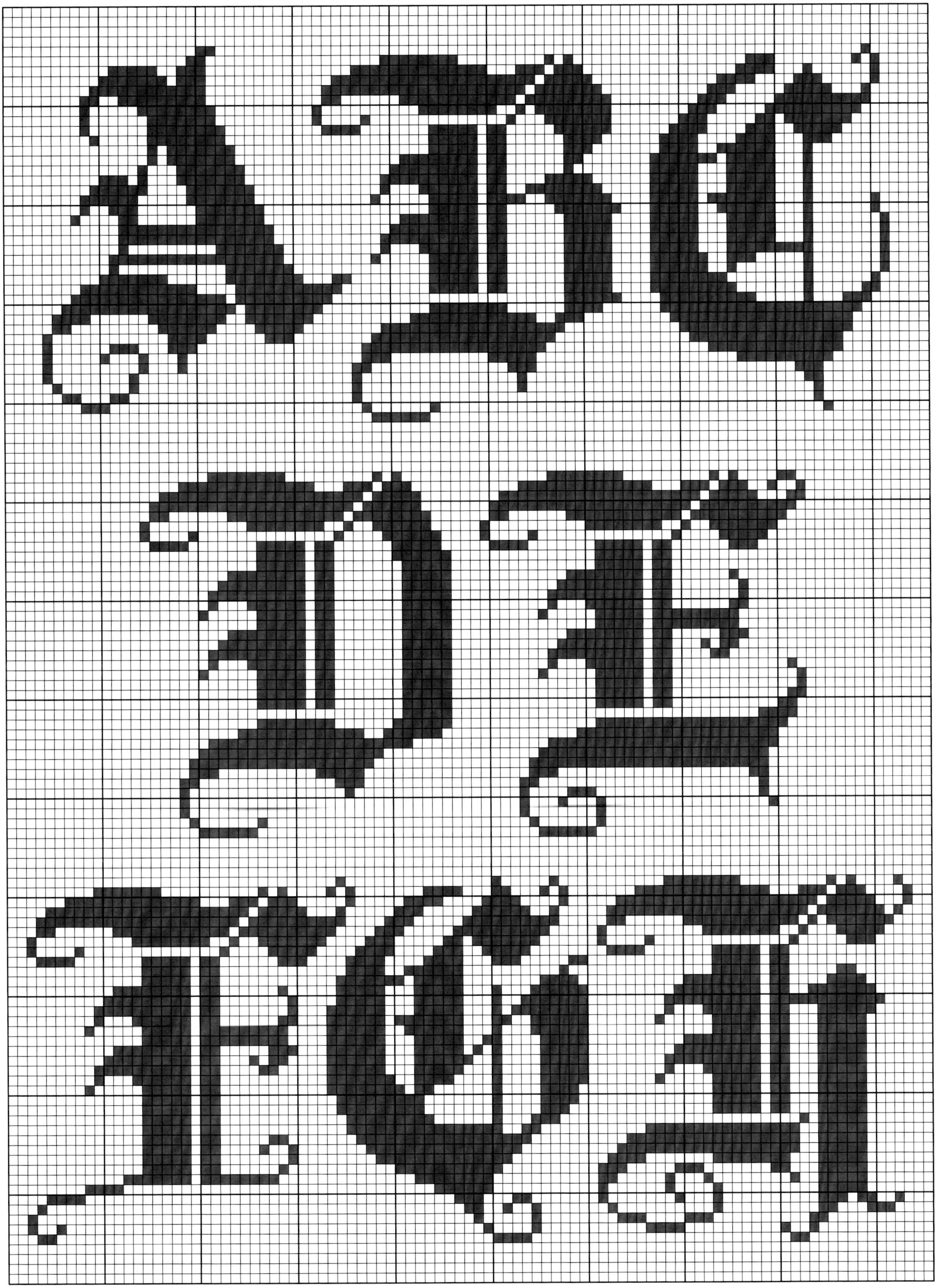

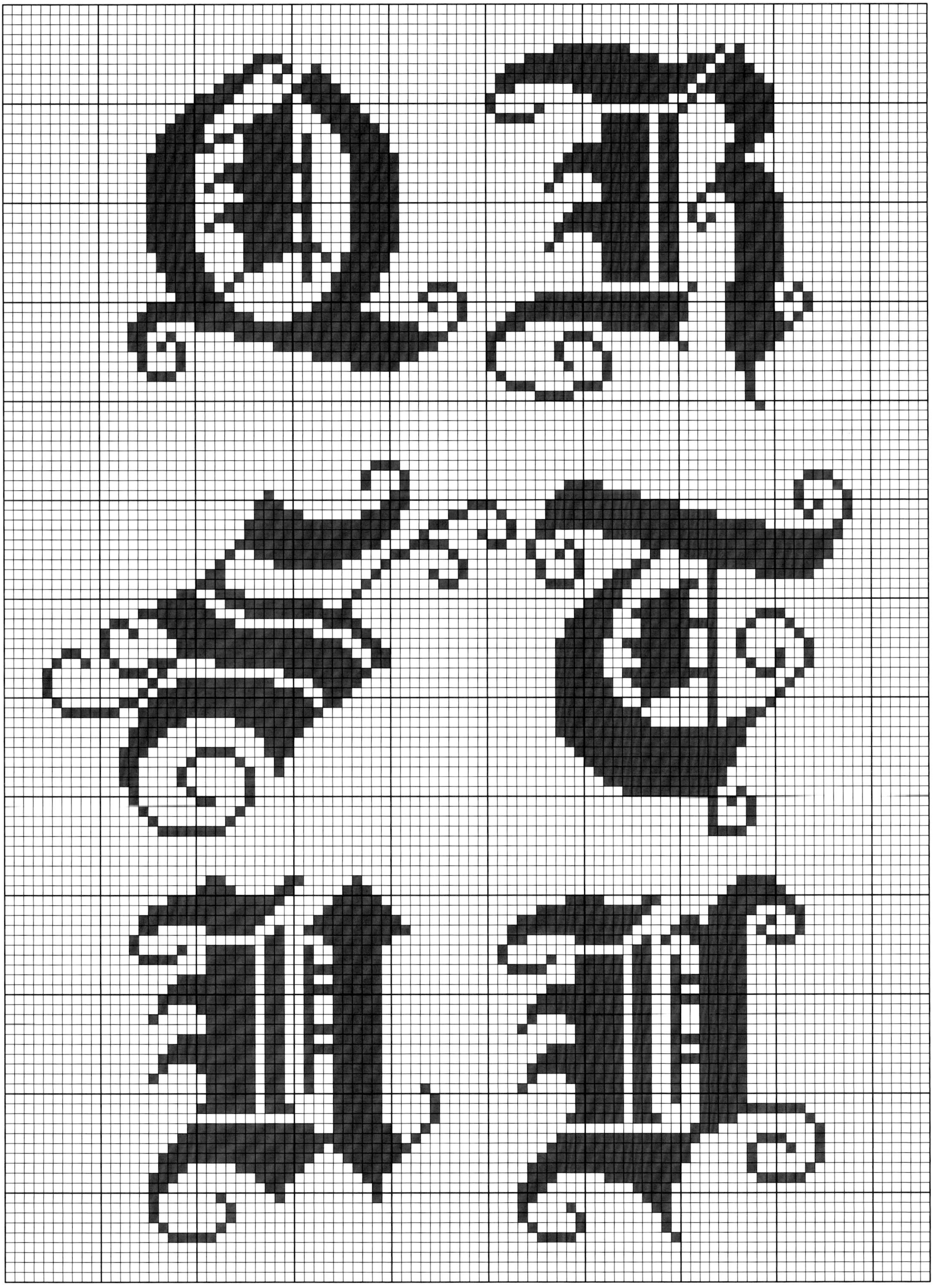

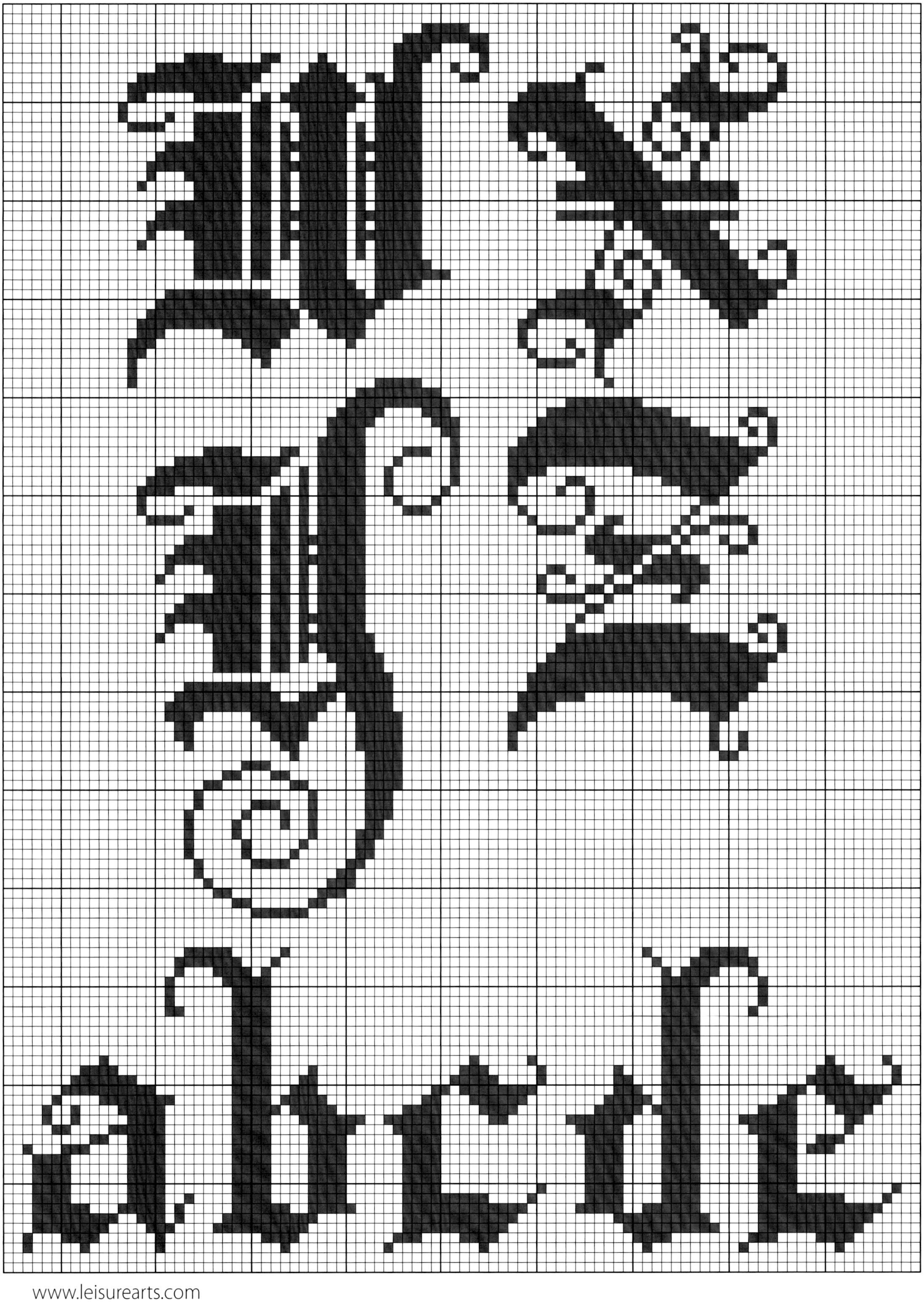

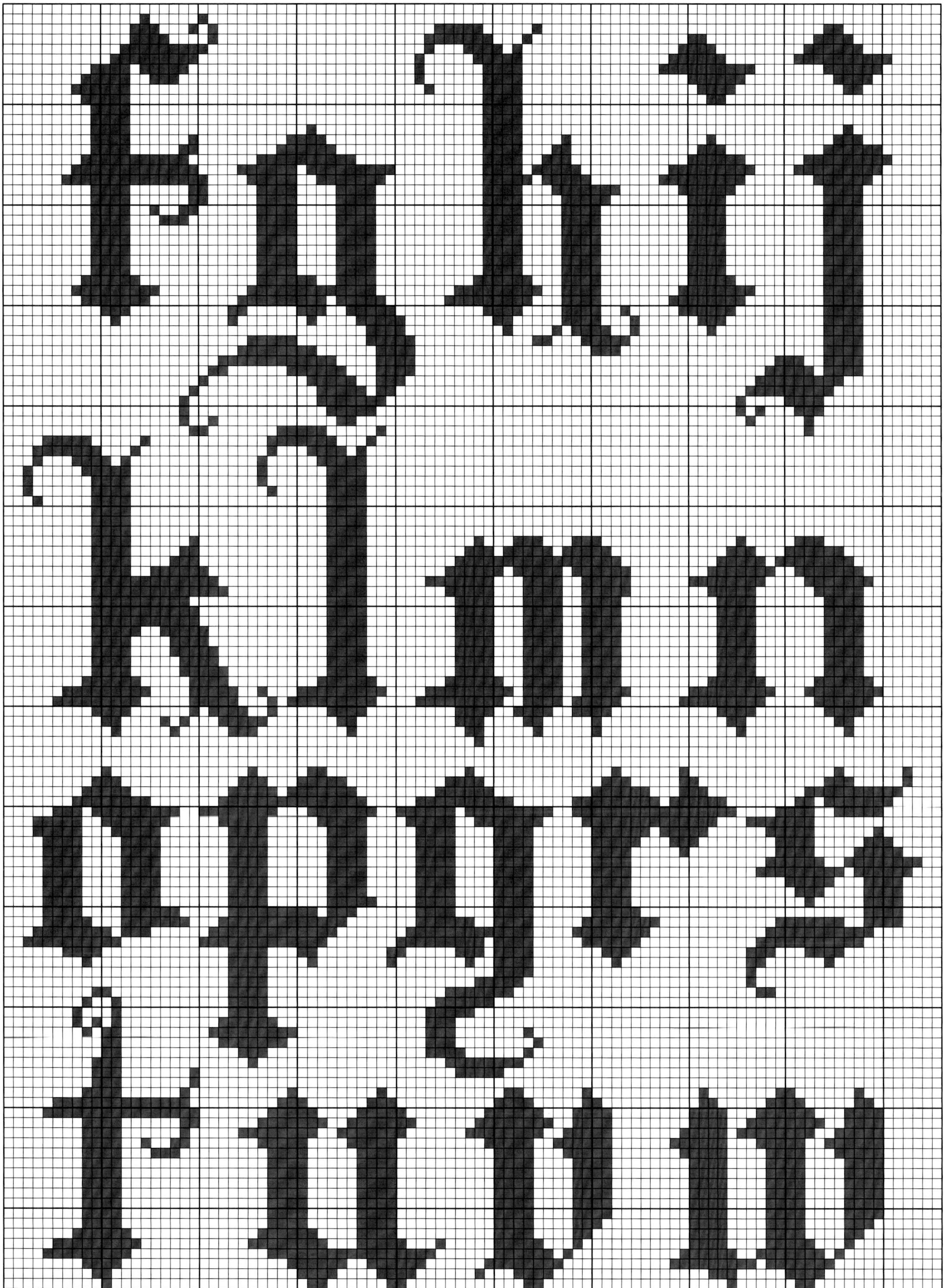

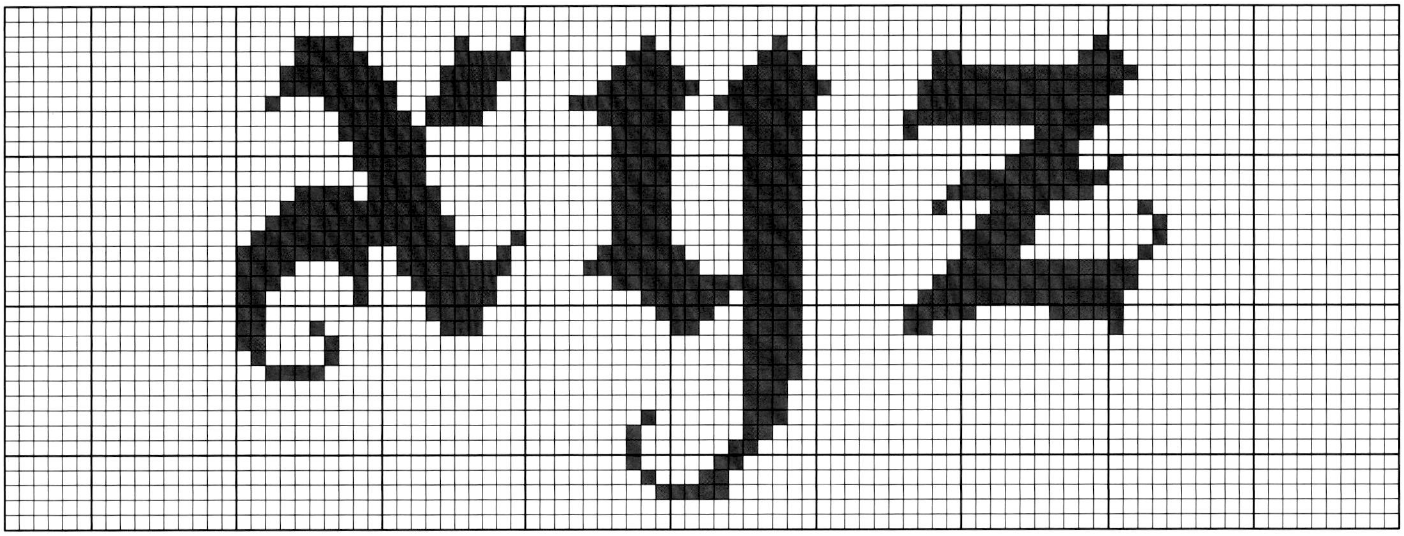
XYZ

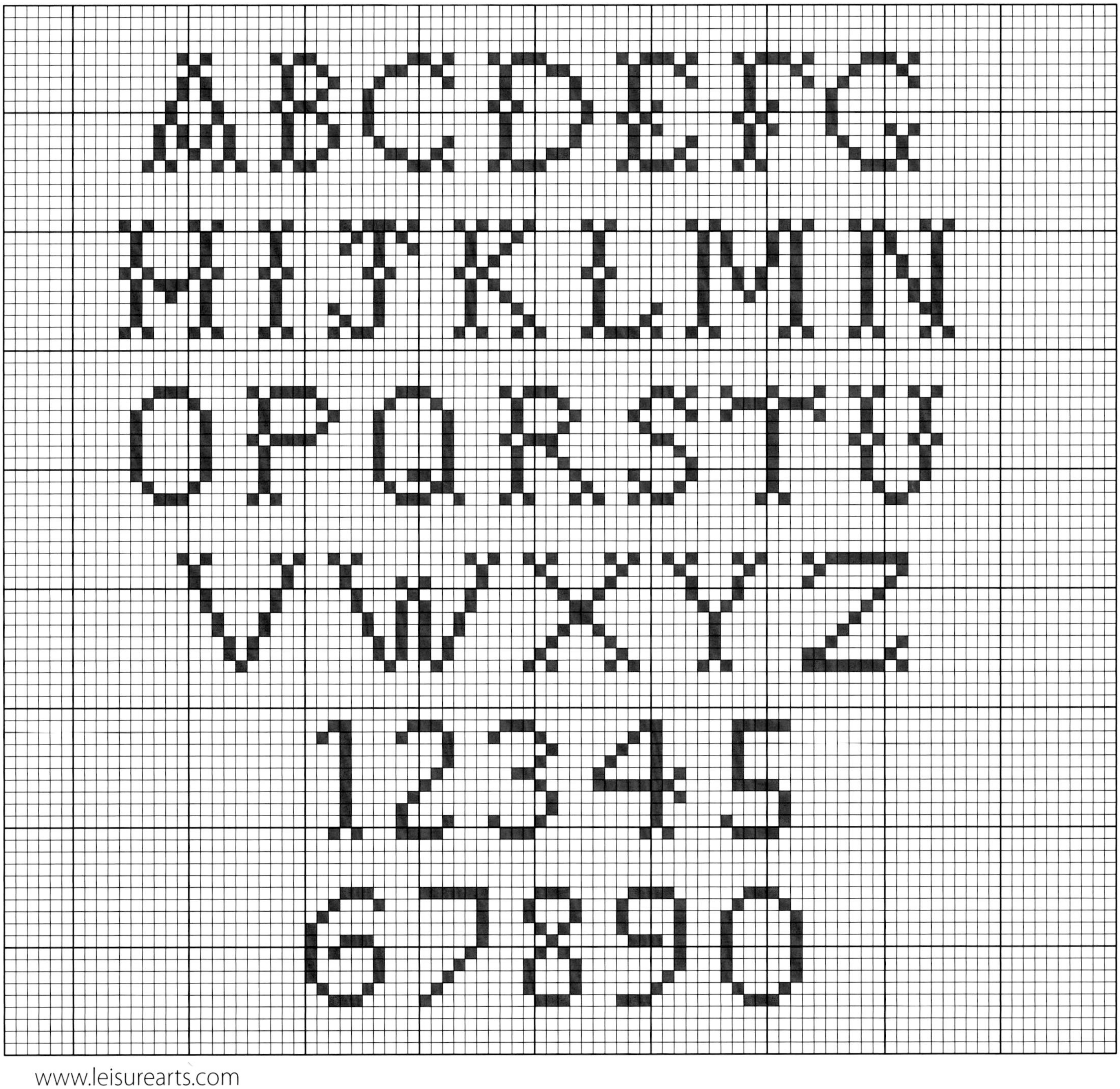
ABCDEFG
HIJKLMN
OPQRSTU
VWXYZ
12345
67890

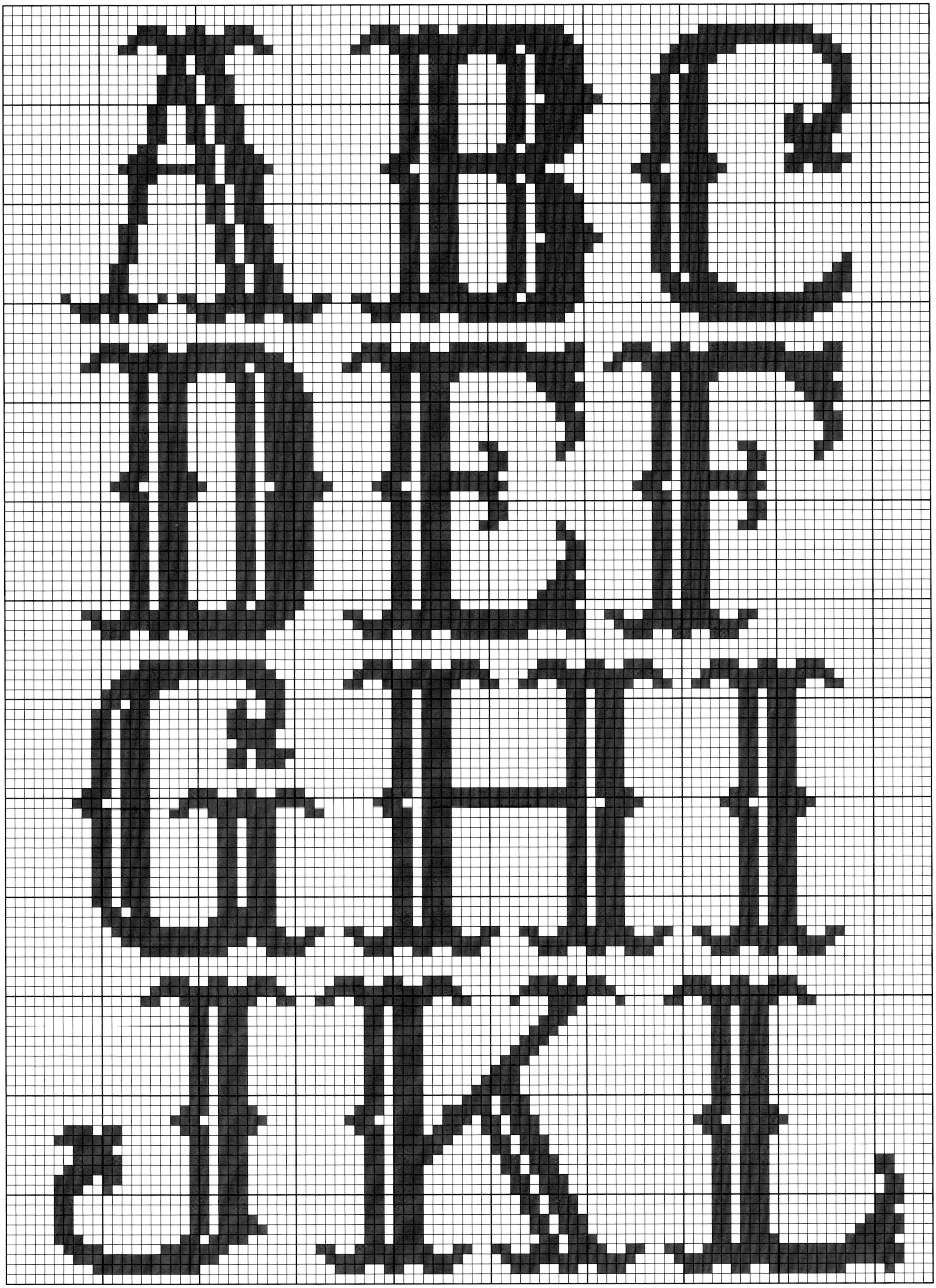
ABC
DEF
GHI
JKL

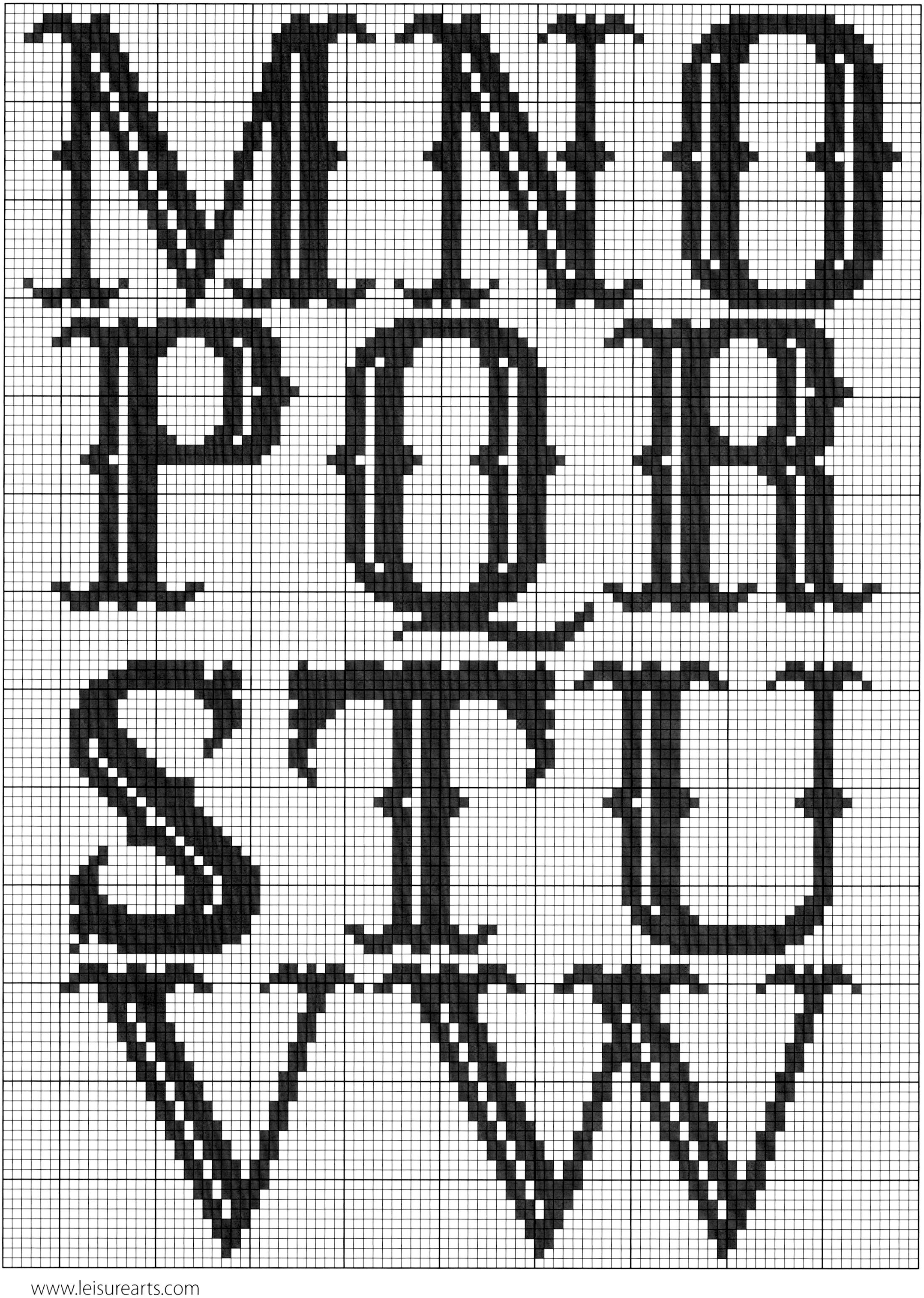
MNO
PQR
STU
VWX

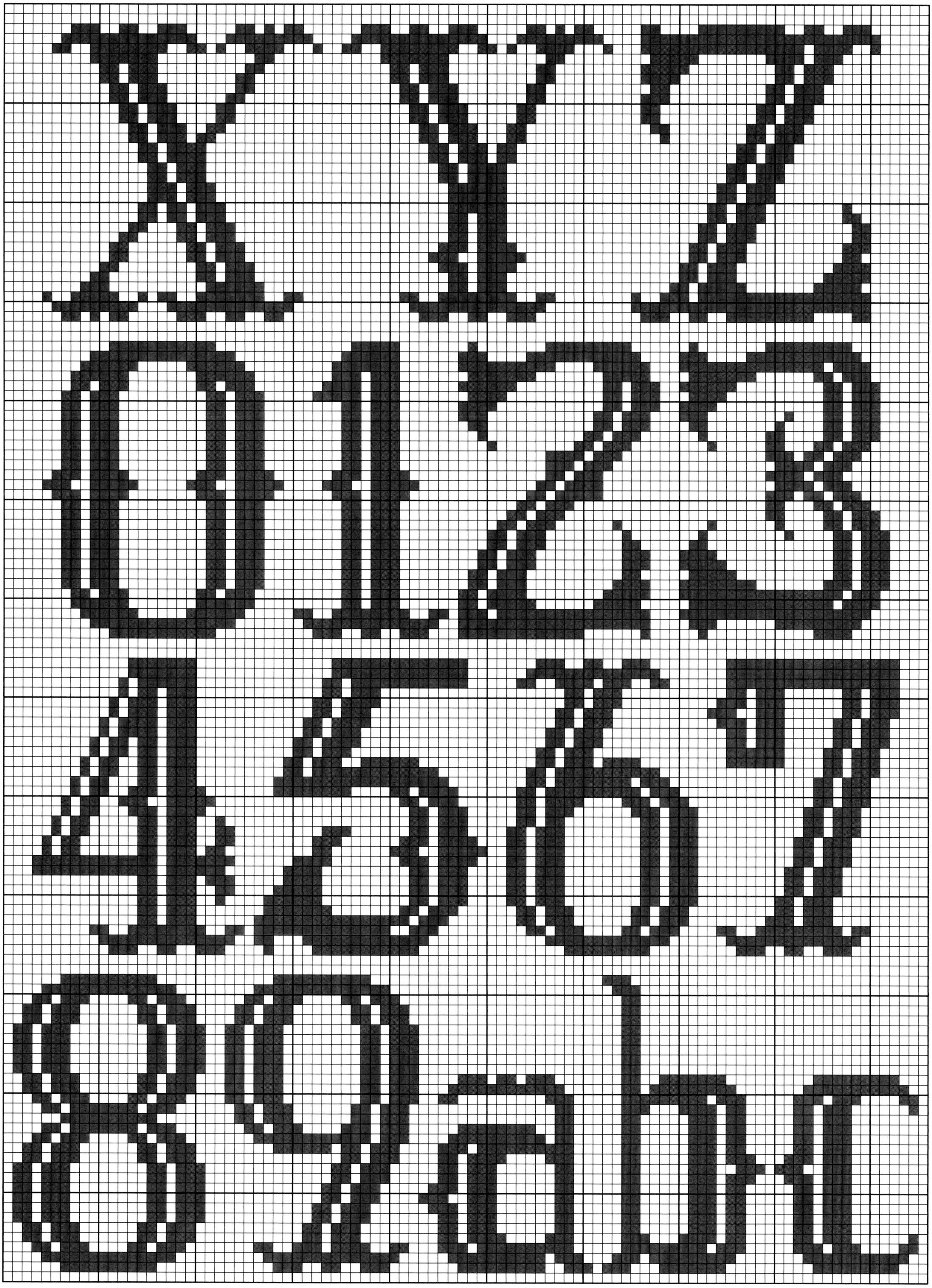

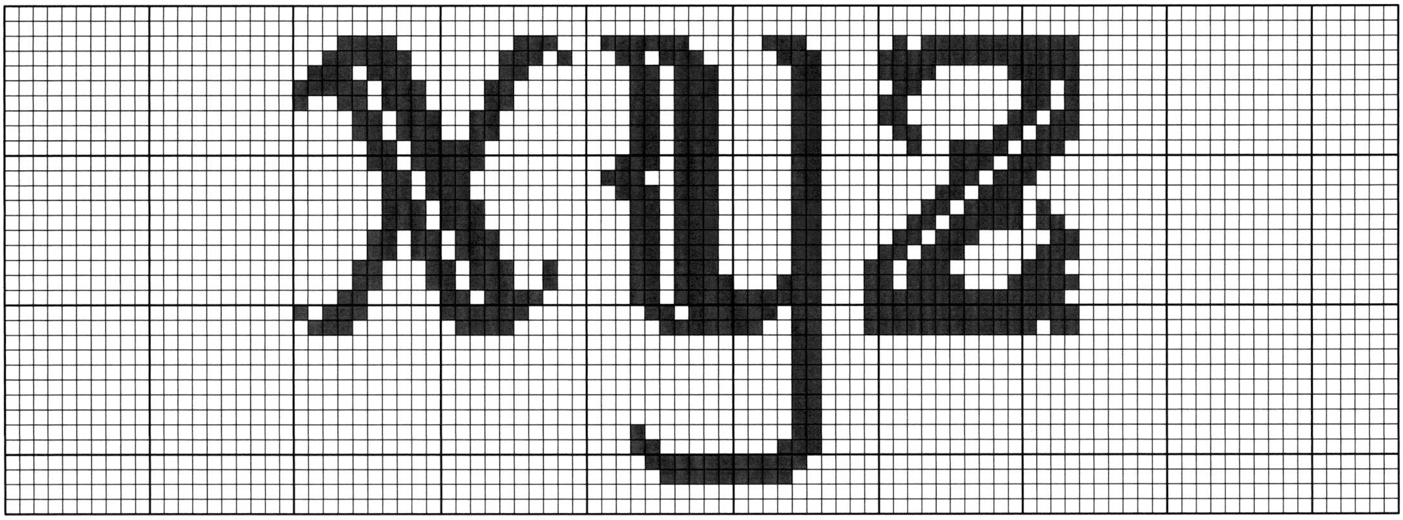

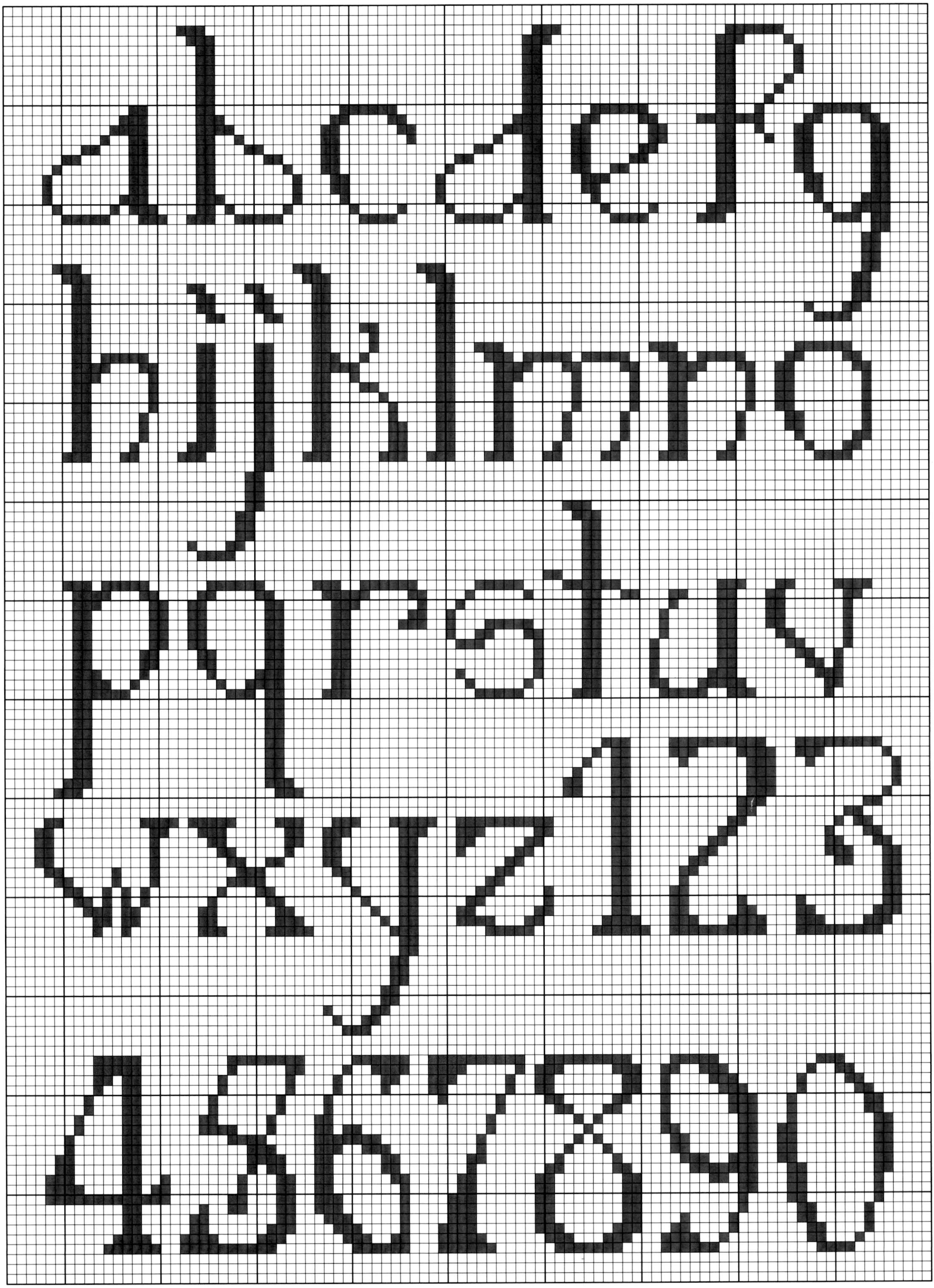
abcdefg
hijklmno
pqrstuv
wxyz123
4567890